A Village Christmas

Personal Family Memories and Holiday Traditions *from*

Thomas Kinkade

Calvin Miller's text published in association with the literary
agency of Alive Communications, 1465 Kelly Johnson Blvd.
#320, Colorado Springs, CO 80920.

Published in Nashville, Tennessee, by Thomas Nelson, Inc.,
Publishers.

Scripture quotations are from THE NEW KING JAMES
VERSION. Copyright © 1979, 1980, 1982, Thomas Nelson,
Inc., Publishers.

ISBN 0-78526960-6

Printed in the United States of America
Bound in Mexico.
2 3 4 5 6 - 04 03 02 01 00

A Village Christmas

Personal Family Memories and Holiday Traditions *from*

Thomas Kinkade

with Calvin Miller

THOMAS NELSON PUBLISHERS
Nashville

Christmas is love, the season of light.

One

Chapter One

The Wonder of Christmas

The coming of Merritt Kinkade was an omen of joy! The year of her birth brought the most memorable Christmas the Kinkades would ever experience. Nineteen eighty-eight was the bright year and Merritt's arrival caused us to breathe the apostle Paul's unforgettable benediction, "Thanks be to God for His indescribable gift!" (2 Cor. 9:15).

Thinking back on this wonderful year, I see it as a time in my life that was marked by a deep need for change. It was as if God made all of 1988 a classroom. I learned that every time we take a significant step in life, God Himself raises some new curtain on our destiny. Be it marriage or children or the launch of a new business, heaven sends what appears to be a happenstance but is actually a concrete opportunity to trust God. So 1988 arrived on schedule with all of its lessons for my life in place. I would never have admitted it at the time, but it was truly a time of finding a new way to serve God in my life.

Several things that year congealed to put me in a spiritually bad frame of mind. The ordinary ups and downs of life were more down than up that year. I, who had always been quite confident, suddenly was attacked by feelings of

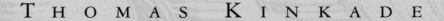

inadequacy. I actually wondered whether—as an artist—I could provide for my family. Throughout the first six years of our marriage it was just Nanette and I, and we had experienced very few worries. But now Merritt Kinkade had entered our world, and while our world was more joyous because of her coming, she brought with her a new trust that I needed to be sure I could provide for all her needs in the years ahead.

Prior to her coming, I had been planning to do some paintings to commemorate our hometown. I wanted to use those paintings to form a new set of art prints that would give the town I so loved a new sense of status in America. I longed to find a way to take my art and give it a very broad appeal. I had always felt that God was the source of my talent—indeed, all talent—but I wanted the world not just to celebrate my art, but Placerville as well. I wanted this town to hold a legitimate place among all those who still treasured good people and sound values. So I began asking God to help me make the great people and lifestyle of my hometown available on a natural basis. If I could gain such wide acceptance, I might feel more secure in my ability to take care of my growing family.

Earlier, both Nanette and I had seen the potential of such a dream, but our trust factor had not grown to the level where we were willing to throw our hearts over the bar and take that great leap of trust in the faithfulness of God.

We doubted the venture. It all seemed so risky. We had been more daring earlier in our lives and at one point

The wonderful thing about Christmas
is that I can reach back into an era gone by
and re-create it in a different time and place.

had taken all of our life savings and created our first print. And thereafter we continued to print our paintings. We achieved a limited success, but now we needed to ask God for something more.

With Merritt's arrival in 1988, I felt a new sense of urgency gathering itself around the word *family*. Merritt was more than just a reminder of grace. Each time I looked at her I knew why the Indian poet Rabindranath Tagore said that every new baby came as proof that God was not yet discouraged with mankind. Merritt was certainly evidence that God had in mind some widening plan for the Kinkades. She was more than a brief stopover in our lives. She was not someone we could cherish for just a few months of her infancy. Her coming made it clear that the word *family* was a lifetime commitment. *Family* required years to write its best definition. It would cost . . . a great deal! It would take the kind of money that even the best artists sometimes didn't make.

The new print I was planning was suddenly strategic. The concept of my ability to be a long-range provider for my family was fearsome, yet gloriously enticing. My fatherly pride soared at the idea of becoming a national artist, but it also trembled at the size of such a dream. But God was bringing me to new self-perception. For the first time I began to see myself as a family man. Merritt had dubbed me with the title *father*.

So I picked up my brushes and palette with a new and growing vision in my life. Gradually a new painting issued forth for the Placerville show. It might have seemed merely a focus on nostalgia to some. But my new way of viewing the world was scrubbed into the very fabric of the canvas. The painting was born and carried in itself a new bit of purpose that was somehow missing from my earlier oils. God and I had become partners in a new life commitment. It had to be that way. Merritt's coming and my new view of myself flowed in the oils of a new commitment to my career.

I called the painting *Christmas on Main Street*. But it was this canvas that forever separated the naive, if eager, young painter from the committed artist, whose paintings became his calling, his light filled way to make the best of America's values thrive in a thousand galleries across the land.

Christmas 1988 arrived in November, a bit early. But the next six weeks visited the Kinkades of Placerville with three marvelous miracles. They were not the kind of miracles one might see on religious cable. They were certainly not the timeless miracles that surface in Luke's wonderful birth narratives. They were ordinary miracles. The kind of common miracles in which God visits us in an insecure moment. You know He is there. You know He has touched you. And you know that when you are forced by the busy affairs of life to leave His presence, you will never be the same again. For He has changed you, and the change is wonderful. We cannot be renovated in mind or heart and not know we have been under the spell of such glorious miracles. But then Christmas is the season of miracles.

During the Christmas season a signature
of love begins to write itself on my wall,
through every nook and cranny of the world.

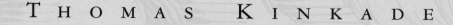

Merritt unquestionably was the central miracle on which the other three were based. The miracle of Merritt gave me a kind of second sight. I could understand why Hannah in the Old Testament would cry out to God, "For this child I prayed." I now realize why Simeon, on seeing the Christ child, cried, "Lord, now You are letting Your servant depart in peace." For Hannah's joy and Simeon's completeness came with Merritt in June of 1988. In her tiny dependency both Nanette and I understood the miracle of Christmas. Mary's baby in a grand way changed all things. In a lesser way Merritt was destined to change all things for us. We did not know how much at the time.

And best of all I could fully comprehend Isaiah's rapture. "For unto us a Child is born." Miracle, indeed! Merritt's birth was Christmas born in the heat of summer, but holding its best lessons for the cold year's end. Merritt had made Christmas of even the most ordinary days, and I could understand why William Cullen Bryant wrote,

O Father, may that Holy star,

Grow every year more bright

And send its glorious beams afar

To fill the world with light.

It is all but impossible to be downcast in the presence of a healthy new baby. Maybe that's why joy is the chief mood of Christmas. What child is this? Why it's God's child. O come let us adore Him!

Thomas Kinkade

My neighborhood at Christmas is

like a fresh landscape of light.

Christmas is the season of a warm heart.

Two

Chapter Two

The First Ordinary Miracle

Christmas on Main Street still stands in the center of our lives. In the future some other painting may hold its pivotal position, but for the moment that canvas is anchored in the center of our years. As Jesus' coming divided time into B.C. and A.D., *Christmas on Main Street* stands at the center of my life. It stands between two Thom Kinkades. The first knew God well. The second trusted Him with everything. The first was capable of worshiping God. The second found the moment-by-moment adoration of God a necessity. ❧

Where is the miracle in all this?

The miracle was that this one painting would change so much about my life. My desires for this painting were twofold. First, I wanted it to succeed to prove to myself that I could actually make a living with my art. Second, I wanted my style of art to say something important about hometown America—about Placerville. Could one painting achieve so much? Was I demanding too much of one canvas? "Could God be trusted to use art to celebrate values and, above all, to provide for the growing Kinkade clan?" was the real question of November 1988.

The painting was to be the central event at a grand unveiling. Unveilings are fraught with a lot of potential and a lot of fears. The curtain falls and then . . . the gasp. The applause. The sudden looking down. Maybe the walking out. The criticism from the critical. The rapture of the adoring. So much hangs in the falling folds of the concealing drapery.

The waiting for the revelation was agonizing. Artists have the "queasies" at such moments, and I was no exception—my anxieties were large indeed. The fleece was out! Would this be the first big step in my career, or was it conceivably the end of my career? I needed it to work. I needed God to prove that He had a real career out ahead of me. I wanted Him to shout loudly when the drapery fell away, "*Starving* isn't the only adjective to be applied to the word *artist*. Your gifts—they're all worthy, for I gave them to you!"

Amazingly, thousands of people showed up at the Placerville Fairgrounds, where the event was held. The veil fell away. *Christmas on Main Street* glistened! The applause was furious, and I felt myself diminished by the raucous endorsements of all who attended. We sold many prints that day, but the sales were not the important part. The important thing was that right there God affirmed my place in His will.

The drapery had fallen. The judgments were in. What was revealed as far as the people could see was *Christmas on Main Street*. But what was really unveiled was a clear sense of the call of God in my life. The word *apocalypse* means

"the revelation." The scholars say that the word literally means "to reveal by drawing back the curtain" as to enable an audience to see a play. God had done just that. He had drawn back the curtains, and my destiny was there before me, clean and free.

I can't remember much else about that wonderful unveiling. I know I was overwhelmed by so many who greeted me to tell me all that my art had meant to their lives. I suddenly realized that already a number of people were collecting my prints and paintings.

Even though *Christmas on Main Street* was not my first print, it was the one by which Placerville affirmed my talent and God spoke to me to secure my future. Indeed, it seemed to point toward the Christmas season just ahead. All of the events were forming a yuletide collage that was distilling into a simple but beautiful miracle. It was an epiphany of joy—a carol of certainty—right in the middle of my life.

One thing that immediately resulted from this epiphany was that I released Nanette from my earlier way of seeing her. I no longer thought, *If my art comes up short, Nanette still has her career; she can provide.* Now I knew I could trust the Great Enabler to supply all things necessary to our home life. Merritt was there, and later there would be others. But however large our family became, Nanette would be a stay-at-home mom.

Think of small rituals of Christmas—

       signatures of love—little touches of

interaction that are unique to the season.

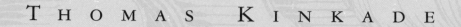

How wonderful was that assurance. So often as a child I left school and came home to an empty house because my mother worked outside the home. Today we call such children *latchkey* kids, but in my day we had no latch or key, so we lived somewhat alone for a part of every day . . . waiting for Mommy. Our children, by the clear leading of God, would have their mommy with them.

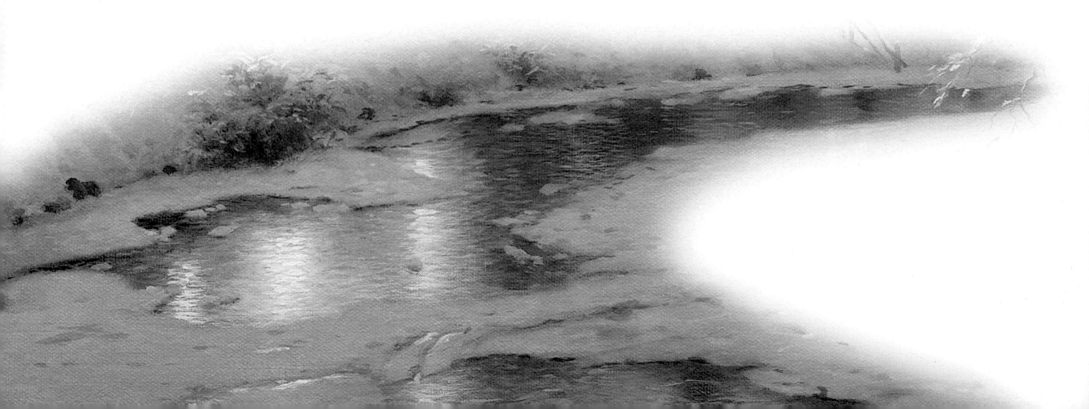

There is no greater gift than the gift of light.

Three

Chapter Three

Early Influences

The ordinary miracle of the Placerville show could never be celebrated as a party for two, God and myself. No, I knew that day all of our lives are built by the world of relationships, which God brings to us. So many people were my mentors and friends. Nanette led the list, but I knew at that Christmas season there were two very special people to whom I owed so much. One was actually at the show, and one was not. ❧

The one who was there was my fourth-grade teacher Mrs. Richards. Her face held a special place among the thousands because I had profited so much from my year as her student. She had caught me one time drawing a caricature of her in class when I didn't think she was looking. I know it did not make her happy, but she seemed to overlook my sketch and see beyond me to what she thought I might become. She never doubted that I would succeed. She often told me that I would become a great artist.

It is not hard to admire those teachers whose affirmations in the lives of their students become self-fulfilling prophecies. She may have been the first person ever to cause me to believe in myself. How appropriate that she should

have been at the Placerville showing.

I remember that she made me see the art that existed throughout the whole world. She taught me to love Mark Twain. She read *Tom Sawyer* to the whole class— this was the first time I encountered the book. In the coming years I would reread *Tom Sawyer* dozens of times. Mrs. Richards saw art everywhere, and her love of literature produced in me a love of excellence wherever it was encountered.

Mrs. Richards! Her very name called me back to my childhood. The debt that children owe is not erased merely because they become adults. Remember Pickwick's counsel: "Happy, happy Christmas, that can win us back to the delusions of our childish days, that can recall to the old man the pleasures of his youth, that can transport the sailor and the traveler, thousands of miles away, back to his own fireside and quiet home." The very name of Mrs. Richards gave such a transport to my spirit at the Placerville show.

She greeted me there, and her cheerful celebration of my life as an artist reminded me how much I owed her. She was truly happy for my success. Her dreams for me had come true. Every prophet rejoices when they live long enough to see their prophecies fulfilled.

The idea of the Christ child is really

phenomenal for children, for it is

the symbol of love and sacrifice.

But there are ghosts of grandeur at the most wonderful celebrations of our lives. These are the happy shades of all—those who forged us and went on or were prohibited from actually being present with us. Glenn Wessels was such a ghost. He was at the Placerville show in everything I had learned or believed about art.

He was the head of the art department at the University of Berkeley campus when we met. How anxious I was to know him and tell him of my esteem for his work. I love spending time with people I admire. When the opportunity presented itself, I knew I had to meet him.

In my early adolescence Glenn Wessels moved to Placerville. I couldn't believe this great artist had picked my hometown to call his hometown. My elation knew no bounds. I introduced myself to Glenn when I was fourteen. It was a brash step for a young kid to even approach such a luminary of the art world. But shyness had never been a quality of mine.

After I presented myself to him, I said, "If you ever need any help around the studio, I would love to help out just for the privilege of being around you." Obviously, it was more my privilege to be around him than vice versa. After I made my offer, he said, "Thanks, sonny, but honestly, I don't have time for you. I'm just too busy."

I was dejected by his refusal, but, more than either of us could know, God already had His hand in the relationship.

Jesus gave joy abundantly—

the aspect of Christmas light—

the expression of God's delight at this season.

By the oddest method of grace—and God's ways are always beyond understanding—an awful, yet wonderful thing happened two years later when I was sixteen. Glenn was involved in a horrible jeep accident with Ansel Adams, the famous photographer. The accident left Glenn badly crippled in the lower part of his body, and he had to walk with a walker for the remainder of his life.

After the accident I once more presented my offer to help him, and this time he gladly accepted. "Thank you, Thomas. I do need help. This is wonderful. What a miracle! Would you mind stretching my canvases and sweeping up the studio from time to time?" Out of his need and my admiration, our relationship was born. I kept the place going, and we talked incessantly of art.

He didn't just talk to me about art, he talked to me about life. He put in my head the vision that artists are the cultural leaders of the world. I began to see what a divine calling art really was. He saw artists as almost a priesthood of sorts, a group of individuals who are remembered past their lifetime. He taught me that, in many ways, artists were the prophets of their times, and their work would be remembered long after the egotistical power plays of the popular politicians of the day had been forgotten. Artists, writers, and thinkers are the ones who really impact the world. They are the true leaders of the culture. Political leaders are poor wanna-bes whose commitment to the avenues of power often

Thomas Kinkade

leave them isolated and forgotten in history. Life goes on, and their impact ebbs.

But artists impact beyond their lifetimes. Look at the writings of Hemingway or the paintings of Mary Cassatt. How influential their lives remain to the very present.

I was apprenticed to Glenn Wessels when I was sixteen. I knew, even as an adolescent, that he was a man of great wisdom. He was eighty years old then, and while he was old enough to be my grandfather, he became for me a kind of surrogate father—a substitutionary dad for the one I never had. He taught me two arts: the art of painting, and the art of making my days count.

The discipline of the second art made possible the release of my talent in the first art. Old age never messed with Glenn's mind, nor did it prevent him from painting well into his eighties. He had suffered the accident, but he vigorously swung his frame along on crutches, never ceasing to paint. Later in life, he would arrive at his studio chasing an aluminum walker, but he never stopped working.

Glenn was a discoverer in life. His style of art was his own, but he never let it lock him into some stolid form that wouldn't attempt a new technique. He was schooled in abstract expressionism and was well-known for his views in the field. But in his later years, he actually left his love of abstraction and became a vital realist.

Christmas is interacting with that

hopefulness that the light might bring us—

an expression of God's love for us.

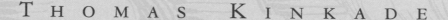

The eye of a true artist sees and enhances and interprets all of life. So it was with Glenn. He painted rocks and trees and all he saw with a brush dipped in intention. During all these years, I continued to admire him. I worked alongside him, stretching his canvases and performing all those routine chores he needed to be done to spread his talent in the world. Stretching his canvases was but a little gift I gave him in comparison with all the gifts he gave me. His primary gift to me was a fascination with art and the life it gave to things that the untrained eye never saw.

Glenn lived in Africa during the Boer Wars, in the early years of the twentieth century. It wasn't just that he traveled everywhere, he personally met the cultural heroes of the century—people I had only read about. He knew Pablo Picasso. He lived in Paris between the world wars, during that seminal period when Ernest Hemingway and Gertrude Stein were holding literary court. F. Scott Fitzgerald, Paul Clay, George Brock, and all the great luminaries of modernism were Glenn's friends.

Glenn, who has been described as one of the most influential teachers in twentieth-century art, was one of the founders of a major art college California College of Arts and Crafts. He knew everybody, was highly influential, and was a critic for the *San Francisco Chronicle*. He was one of the great thinkers on the importance of art culturally and on the trends of art as an expression of humanity.

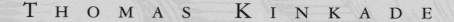

And he was my friend. In some ways he—through the unseen hand of my heavenly Father—was creating me. He brought my own unique gifts to serve in ways that neither he nor I suspected at the time. But this colossus of experience and wisdom was my mentor from early adolescence.

They say that Paderewski never played the piano for his great audiences. He always assumed his teacher was in the audience and always played for him. I felt as though I were onstage at the Placerville show and playing for my teacher. How grateful I was for such a life.

So the day of the Placerville showing, even though Glenn Wessels was not present, he was in the audience. Even as the veil fell from the painting, I knew that this celebration was as much for him as for anyone actually present. His unseen nod of pleasure was the best part of the ordinary miracle of 1988.

But beyond Glenn Wessels' influence on my life, I knew that 1988 was the year that God made us into a family, and after the show, Nanette and I readied ourselves for Christmas. Van Dyke's great Christmas benediction could easily have been written just for us.

Father of all men, look upon our family

Kneeling together before thee

And grant us a true Christmas.

—Henry Van Dyke, "A Christmas Prayer for the Home"

Creativity is essentially an act

of discovery, an act of faith.

Light is an evocative force within a painting
of a life. It is at once energizing and calming.

Four

Thomas Kinkade

Chapter Four

The Second Ordinary Miracle

The Placerville show was Christmas come early. But a second miracle followed hard upon it. It snowed. No, it didn't just snow—it was a blizzard. Was this possible? Snow in Placerville? In all the time I had lived there, even growing up there, it had never snowed on Christmas. And this one came, not exactly on Christmas, but close enough that it seemed fair to count it as Placerville's only white Christmas. Glorious, heavy, wet snow snuggled in the unwilling arms of the trees breaking off some of the limbs. ❧

The snow itself was a miracle only because it beckoned me most powerfully to go cross-country skiing right in Placerville. I'm not sure what the neighbors must have thought (the Kinkades have never been predictable people). I took Merritt, put her in her little backpack, strapped her to my back, and introduced my wide-eyed six-month-old to cross-country skiing.

I skied right out of the front door of our home. It was the first and only time that ever happened, and Merritt was delighted. It seemed that she and I literally skied into the Christmas season. With the warmth of the Placerville

show still gilding my mind, this seemed to be my first real Christmas. And even if I had known better seasons, it was definitely Merritt's first Christmas.

A baby long ago had started Christmas, and our own baby spoke to the glory of Christmas. I looked at our little Merritt. She was so small, so dependent. But she had been like a new dawn in our family, and I could understand why Van Dyke said of the infant Christ that His birth was the sunrise of the Bible.

Out, out, out of the driveway and into the odd, ill-fitting, uncustomary winter wonderland. The new powder, too heavy to be real powder, glistened in the sun and paved our tracks with sparkling sunlight. I talked to Merritt, as parents will, while we skied together. She cuddled against my parka, sometimes drooling with delight and sometimes gurgling odd replies to my unceasing flow of chatter.

I skied out toward Hoovers Farm. In later years, Merritt and her siblings learned to love this place. They loved the farm animals and delighted in feeding the pigs, horses, cows, and chickens. The Hoovers also had an aviary full of all kinds of birds on the farm. Kenneth Grahame wrote in *Wind in the Willows*:

Who were the first to cry Nowell?

Count your blessings—

only when you do will you realize

how many you have.

THE SECOND ORDINARY MIRACLE

Animals all as it befell,

In the stable where they did dwell!

Joy shall be theirs in the morning.

The snow produced a sense of euphoria. And the animals at Hoovers Farm were properly in their place to form a Placerville nativity. All that was wanting was the Christ child, and He was there in abundance in my heart as I reckoned with God in the new snow.

Soon I found that I had quit talking with Merritt and had begun talking with God. My mind savored the memories and the moment. With God's marvelous miracle of life squirming in her backpack, I knew that the Kinkades were going to have a wonderful Christmas. Even as Merritt blinked wide-eyed into the sunlight, the euphoria of God's care and love for us was mine. I skied with a lightness of being one rarely feels in life.

The ski trip caused me to remember that paradise is what you make of it at the time you are creating it. God had made a whole landscape of white, and Merritt and I were literally skiing through the artistry of God. We are God's creation, and the glory is that we are most like Him when we begin to create. God must have beamed with satisfaction

over Eden, for what He had created was indeed perfect.

Merritt hung on my back as I skied through an inner dialogue of years. Placerville or anywhere else can be an Eden to the eye of who will see it. Depending on God to create that world is something that has become so innate to me that I am amazed as I've read the biographies of other artists who did not depend on Him.

Case in point: Edward Hopper was one of my real heroes. He would average three paintings a year. His wife related that months would go by when he wouldn't produce a painting. That is evidence of a lack of faith. When I sit down in front of any canvas and move my arm, I don't care if I am discouraged or frustrated. It doesn't matter whether or not I even feel like painting at the moment, the inspiration of God arrives right on time, and it is pretty clear that the inspiration is from above. A Christian artist always invites the participation of God. He may now and then experience a dead time. Some might call this an artist's block. But the artist whom God guides never suffers from it. For artist's block is soon remedied by the great God who is never out of creativity. If the artist continues to act and trust and keeps working, God, his collaborator in the artistic endeavor, will show up and breathe creativity through his craft once again.

Eventually the canvas gets covered, eventually the world emerges, and a rich new reality is born. God owns the day!

Resist the pressures of those who would

prefer you to walk in the ruts.

Climb outside your box! Live!

The artist and his Creator rejoice together. God alone had made the great canvas of the Placerville winter wonderland. The snow was glorious! The sun was wonderful! Merritt was beautiful!

Placerville, wearing her miracle cloak of white, was exactly the right geography for such a morning of contemplation. Merritt and I skied on for what seemed forever. The unveiling of my art at Placerville some weeks before reminded me that the God of the Christmas snow was the God who worked miracles in my life. When I painted, I knew it was God who was doing it and not me. His love passes through the hands of an artist and awakens the talent to its finest self. The contemplation during that ski trip reminded me that my art would always yield to His assurance. There I would paint, there I would ski, there I would live out the responsibility of my calling.

Merritt sagged heavily in the backpack; she was sound asleep as I skied back to the house. Even seeing my house caused me to thank God for a Christian home.

The true Christmas miracle is that all of us—in each of our circumstances, big or small—have to thank God for the ordinary miracles of Christmas every day. After all, God is the meaning of life. God is the source of new life and hope, as His light ever emanates into a needy, dark world. Only as I skied back into my yard did I notice that earlier I had put up Christmas lights outside. I smiled as I thought that I had done it "for Merritt."

I have found there is something about

being in the snow in sunlight that is

brighter than anything else in the world.

Somehow I had convinced myself that this little six-month-old child was going to appreciate them.

As I took off the skis, I thought of just how far God had brought me. Had I actually put up lights for a little baby? It must be so. Here was more evidence that the artist had turned into a family man—the artist who at Berkeley had once considered himself a rather bohemian free spirit, wanting no encumbrances on his life. Now all of a sudden, this secular, once worldly-wise artist had traded his Paul Gaugin beret for a Leave-It-To-Beaver ball cap! Jesus, who once changed water into wine, had changed a libertarian into a father.

I pried Merritt out of the backpack and laid her on the bed. God be praised! I really was different. I had Christmas lights—I was a family man! God be praised also for the snow that led me in one short ski trip back to the center of myself. And I was delighted to discover that I, who had once been self-centered, now had a wonderful Lord at the center. This Lord who had long ago worked miracles all over Palestine had visited me in Placerville and worked an authentic and yet ordinary miracle.

When we were shut in for the night, I settled down before the fire a very blessed man. The door was bolted, the fireplace roared, and the smile of God was all about me in the room. The words of that happy Christmas quatrain were mine:

The door is on the latch tonight,

The hearthfire is aglow.

I seem to hear soft, passing feet—

The Christ-child in the snow.

—Anonymous

The miracle snow of Placerville was already thawing. But the miracle of that day was more enduring than the snow.

This gold was mine—a day of dialogue with God was His instruction for a lifetime.

During this wondrous season the very

       environment is shaped by the loving hand of

Christmas itself—a transformation

       seems to happen on its own.

The concept of love, the true gift
of Christmas, is the gift of light.

Five

Chapter Five

The Third Ordinary Miracle

In 1988 we owned a small house situated on ten acres that had once been part of a larger ranch. It sat on a hill, and I would like to tell you that it was one of those grand Victorian houses, which I was so fond of painting. Unfortunately it was not. But it was well-situated, and from our back porch, on a clear day, it seemed you really could see forever. 🌹

Nanette and I would sit up there all year long and watch the lights come on at night. As I sat on my back porch in December surveying the lights, I thought of how Mrs. Richards had read to us of Huck Finn. Huck once went up on a hill to look over St. Petersburg. In the valley below him, Huck saw the lights and speculated on what those lights in the wee small hours of the morning meant. He reasoned that some folks were up late with sick friends or relatives. He felt that others were just getting up early to get a head start on their work in the fields.

John Milton long ago described the view of lights like those my eyes beheld:

Peaceful was the night

Wherein the Prince of Light

His reign of peace upon the earth began.

There must be some almighty relationship between peace and perspective. No sooner did I see the whole of Placerville in lights than I had a feeling of peace. There was light. God was in charge. All must be right with His world.

I wondered about Placerville! The lights of the town seemed to be stars that opted to spend the night in the valley. But the lights were all that was to be seen. By day we could see individual homes from our vista. By day telephone lines and roads cut the city up into odd, selfish segments of life. But by night all that could be seen was a field of lights.

At night, Placerville became an odd starscape of some random electrical grid work. The divisions were all gone, the ugly separateness of highways and railroad tracks was gone. The night had forged a community of oneness out of all of those lights.

I knew that was why Jesus came. He wanted to end the ugly separateness and to build a giant communion of people who loved one another and for whom there were no boundaries. He was indeed the man for all human beings. Jesus

The thing I love about snow and painting

is that it's essentially a reflective surface;

I really have fun bringing light onto

snow from such things as windows and lamps.

Snow gives me a chance to play with light.

was the miracle by which God became touchable. He was like God, but then one would expect that of God's Son. The really great miracle was that He was also like us. Donald English wrote that Jesus was as much like us as God could be. And because He came in the flesh, He made God and heaven itself accessible to us. That's why Dyer wrote, "Christ uncrowned himself, to crown us, and put off his robes to put on our rags . . . he came from heaven to earth that he might send us from earth to heaven."

In short, Christ came, Christmas too, to make the world a home for one family who would believe in the Christ of Christmas. I was eager that this should be my definition of home. *Home.* Why was this word so important to me? I had once been a boy who thought he wanted to get as far away from home as possible.

That impact on me as a young boy fueled my need to get away. I lived in a different area of Placerville at that time. When I left, I had this deep need to get away, to see a broader world, to shake the dust of Placerville off my feet. Out of convenience, my wife and I came back to Placerville because Nanette's parents, who were building a house, ended up moving overseas to take a job offer. We were able to buy their home without any financing. It was a marvelous thing! That purchase made our decision to move back to Placerville.

But it wasn't until that Christmas that I looked down on those lights and thought to myself, *Those lights are*

Nothing is more effective than to give
presents that are an expression of yourself.

blinking inside the homes of our friends and families. And just look at the number of those blinking lights.

The thought occurred to me, *Yes, the little boy has come home.* Home is, as one sage said, the place that when you go there they have to take you in. I now felt again that Placerville was truly my home. My roots had changed. My desire to wander was over.

This was the Christmas when a great idea burst in my heart. I decided to become the painter of light. Those lights I saw in the valley were the very lights that burned in every home through the hearts of the people who love one another. It was then that Matthew 5:16 was crystallized in my heart: "Let your light so shine before men, that they may see your good works and glorify your Father in heaven." Each of us is a purveyor of light. Each of us must let our light shine before men. Each of us must let others see our good works and glorify our Father in heaven. I also thought of the child's hymn that encourages us to let our light shine so that it warms the life of another. I suddenly saw my art as a tool that I could use to bring God's light into other homes.

My own small talent was a little light that burned in my house—a little candle of joy to be shared with a lot of people. The success of the print that year had made all of that clear. All of a sudden I began to see that people would want what I was painting. They would be drawn to it. The little boy who had suddenly become a man had a vision in

St.
Nicholas
Circle

Welcome Friends
Old and New
Linger Here
A Day or Two

POP:
A FEW
KINDLY SOULS

Thomas
Kinkade

Gingerbread

Set oven to 325 degrees
Bake time 50-55 minutes
2 1/3 cup all-purpose flour (do not use self-rising flour)

1/2 cup shortening
1/3 cup sugar
1 cup molasses
3/4 cup hot water
1 teaspoon baking soda
1 teaspoon ground ginger
1 teaspoon ground cinnamon
3/4 teaspoon salt
1 large egg

Grease bottom and sides of a 9x9 pan and lightly flour. Beat all ingredients with electric mixer on low speed for about 30 seconds, scraping bowl constantly. Pour into pan. Bake until toothpick comes out clean. Serve warm.

his heart, a passion. Art was not just to make money or pay the bills. It was not just to make one famous or rich, but to be used by God to let His light shine before everyone in such a way as to draw people to His love.

Somewhere in the galaxy of lights far below were the lights of our church. How we loved it. Its people were our friends. It was a little hometown church—very much like the little country church I was raised in. Even as I saw it, I knew we would be there on Christmas Eve celebrating with our friends the God who came in human flesh to make hope and peace possible.

Christmas

When Christmas actually arrived, the events of the earlier weeks had conditioned me to look for miracles with a keener eye than I once would have done. Miracles are all around us. Those who train their inner vision will see nothing but miracles in the season of Christ's birth.

Except for the outside lights I had put up, I had to admit that the house we lived in was not very traditional. It was not the kind of house I ever put on canvas—not a Victorian turret or a filigreed eave to be seen. Still the plain old

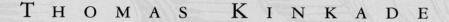

house probably had served as an impetus to my painting. It was so very average that it goaded me into painting

Victorian houses because of their form of whimsical architecture. Ours was just a simple house; it didn't have the charm

that I wished it had. But I suppose that might have been said about the stable in Bethlehem. God needs no mighty

architecture to do mighty things.

All of us are more blessed by what is missing in our lives than by what is present. Those artists who were most

famous for painting the Rocky Mountains were often people from back east who adored the crags of Colorado and fan-

tasized them right onto their canvases. So what if our little house lacked interest? My own vision of life could build a

great Christmas on what wasn't there—except in our hearts.

The first miracle that I remember that Christmas Eve was the smell of hot ginger wafting through our simple

home. My wife is famous for her gingerbread, and she loves to bake it. Gingerbread is like coffee at an outside, early

morning campfire. It is difficult to tell if the real joy is in the smelling of it or in the consuming of it.

With Nanette's gingerbread, my mind was visited by the Ghost of Christmas Past. My grandmother on my

father's side was quite a character. She always read western novels and lived in a tiny mobile home. It was filled with

piles of old books, all of which she had read at one time or another. In her younger years, she had served as a fry cook

Seeking light is the most basic

and universal human impulse.

on a passenger train. She thought she was a better cook than my brother and I esteemed her to be. In fact, we didn't at all like the way she cooked bacon and eggs, but she was a stocky German-Irish woman to whom no one in the world ever said no. So we ate what she cooked for us.

Her best quality was that she lived near Disneyland, so however much we hated her cooking, eating it was a small price to pay for the privilege of visiting her—and more important, visiting Disneyland. I've always felt bad that I did not stop and spend more time with her while she was alive. But children are often bent on some petty agenda that sees old people as not very interesting.

We have used our Christmases to remedy that situation for our own children. Their grandparents come to us and we go to them all through the Christmas season. I know the power of good, godly grandparents, and I want that power to play a strong moral role in the development of my children's values.

When a grandparent is a person of faith, they have the ability to impact a child like none other. I notice that our children's grandparents are never preachy and are always available to listen and counsel them through the rough parts of life. When grandparents love the Lord, they are the artists and architects of noble destiny.

We joined our church friends at the Christmas Eve service, and the joy of it was wonderful. I thought of Gruber's

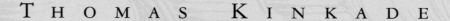

Silent Night. Then the lingering strain from *We Three Kings* echoes in the clear bright skies over Placerville and causes me to think of that "star of wonder, star of night, star with royal beauty bright," which must have made the Bethlehem skies seem a gorgeous planetarium, baffling Herod and delighting the Magi.

Christmas Eve services ring with a camaraderie that is only truly available once a year. So it was with the service in Placerville. Of course, there are church members who are never really very nice to one another. But there is never a single Scrooge present on Christmas Eve. The *bahs* and *humbugs* are all *glorias* somehow. No lurking *Grinch* ever steals a Christmas Eve service. We left the church to return home, cuddling our child and understanding just why it was that the whole world got so excited about a baby. It was Merritt's first year, and what she had added to our lives was all *in excelsis Deo*. In God's eyes, babies are always *in excelsis Deo*. All babies gain a special sanctity at Christmas.

Long ago, between 1534 and 1584, the good citizens of Coventry performed a Christmas pageant on the steps of Coventry Cathedral. When they came to the part where the wicked King Herod was massacring the infants of Bethlehem, they sang a lament for the babies who died so that the infant Christ could live. The words to the song still celebrate that haunting Christmas theme:

The best kind of adjectives I use to

describe Christmas, I also use to define my

life—simplicity, values, family, home, and

old-fashioned kinds of things.

THE THIRD ORDINARY MIRACLE

Lul-lay, thou little tiny Child,

Bye-bye, lul-loo, lul-lay.

Lul-lay, thou little tiny Child,

Bye-bye, lul-loo, lul-lay.

It is marvelous to me that so many little babies died so that, in all the ages to come, the Baby that actually survived the Bethlehem massacre might die so that all could live. A lullaby was God's long-term method of saving all of us. Mary's Baby would, in time, make eternity safe for all of God's children.

We worshiped our Savior, and His almighty presence was easy to behold among our friends as we praised Him on that Christmas Eve. *He* was worthy, and He was Lord and in each one of us *adored*. I knew that Christians throughout all time had gathered on Christmas Eve to praise the condescension of God, who in Paul's words, "did not consider it robbery to be equal with God, but made Himself of no reputation, taking the form of a bondservant, and coming in the likeness of men. And being found in appearance as a man, He humbled Himself and became obedient to the point of death, even the death of the cross" (Phil. 2:6–8). The great God—a baby? Jesus, the crowned monarch of

heaven, as small as our little Merritt? Who could doubt God's love at Christmas? Who would not honor God for the glory of His condescension at Bethlehem?

This was the event beyond all events. No wonder Ignazio Silone made his famous remark on the meaning of Christmas. When asked what the most important date was in Western history, he unhesitatingly replied, "December 25, the year ZERO." *Adeste Fideles* is the only response of the faithful when they think of the marvelous work of God at Bethlehem.

The idea of Christmas is a wonderful thing. Approach it as creatively as you can and show love for those you care about.

Six

Chapter Six

Family Celebrations

We were all too soon back from our time of worship. From the larger family of God, we returned to the celebration of our own family. One of the traditions my mom instituted was to bake wiener roll-ups for dinner on Christmas Eve. Nanette and I had kept her tradition alive. Gingerbread and wiener roll-ups—it may not sound like eggnog and plum pudding, but in all my years of this fare, I have never suffered a stomachache! ❧

Christmas is always a blending of two different families. As families blend, traditions merge and become a kind of invitation to start our own traditions. So after dinner on that Christmas Eve, Nanette and I and little Merritt read "The Night Before Christmas," then we turned in our Bibles to see what Luke had to say about the first Christmas. One of the new traditions that has become so special to us is the baking of a "Happy Birthday, Jesus" cake. When we began this tradition, we had no idea how important it would become to our children in the years to follow.

Nanette and I also established a tradition in our house that dates back to when I was a little boy. As children we

Hot Spiced Tea

1 teaspoon whole cloves
1 1-inch cinnamon stick
6 cups water
2 1/2 tablespoons black tea
3/4 cup orange juice
2 tablespoons lemon juice
1/2 cup sugar

Add spices to water. Heat to boiling. Add tea, steep for 5 minutes. Strain. Heat fruit juices and sugar just to boiling. Stir. Add to hot tea.
Makes 6-8 servings.

always got to open a token present on Christmas Eve. (Sometimes we opened more than one, if we really put the pressure on our parents!) Christmas Eve was a big time for us. I think Mom knew she would have two insomniacs on her hands if she made us wait for all the presents until Christmas Day.

So, many years later, Nanette, Merritt, and I also each open a trivial present which only whets our appetites to what bigger things await us in the morning. Full of gingerbread and wiener roll-ups, we fall asleep. No visions of sugarplums dance in our heads. But what reigns in our hearts is the knowledge that Christmas 1988 had set the course for our journey into life. And when God's will is followed, every day is Christmas and every evening the night before Christmas.

When Christmas Day arrived, I gave three gifts. The first gift I gave was the building of a warm fire. In the woodstove down in my studio, I had perfected the art of building a fire. I could agree easily with all of Dickens's assumptions that a Christmas fire is the most important element of Christmas, in some ways. The hearth has always been the altar of the Kinkade Christmas. I take great pride in building a fire. Maybe because I grew up in a home without a fireplace, I treasure, all the more, a blazing hearth. Pickwick knew the joy of it:

THOMAS KINKADE

"This," said Mr. Pickwick, looking around him, "this is indeed comfort."

"Our invariable custom," replied Mr. Wardle.

"Everyone sits down with us on Christmas Eve, as you see them now—servants, and all; and here we wait till the clock strikes twelve to usher Christmas in, and while away the time with forfeits and old stories. Trundle, my boy, rake up the fire."

Up flew the bright sparks in myriads as the logs were stirred, and the deep red blaze sent forth a rich glow, that penetrated the farthest corners of the room, and cast its cheerful tint on every face.

"Come," said Wardle, "a song—a Christmas song."

I found myself celebrating Wardle's advice. Who can build a Christmas fire without a carol on his lips, even as the sulfur matches make the sparks fly?

And so it was as I sang a lilting carol—not quite aloud, I think—as my Christmas 1988 yuletide pyromania took control. The fire roared against the cold room till the orange shadows of the fireplace battled the little lights on the tree, and the fire won.

I can easily paint Christmas in July

       because of my love for extravagant fantasies—

fantasies are always determined by what's

       missing in our lives—Christmas, too, fills up

what's missing in our lives.

Merritt was soon crawling around on the floor, excited for reasons she could not understand at the moment. But the fire symbolized for us that Christmas what John of the Cross had called the Flame of Divine Love. It is the love of God that must warm the home. It is that flame which is unquenchable in the life of every family. God's love burned all through our Christmas season. Yes, that fire was my first, and maybe my best, Christmas gift that season and every year since then.

But there were more gifts to come. For Merritt, I had bought a beautiful little rocking horse. It was her first important toy. It was, perhaps, just as important that I give it to her for I was a new convert to responsible familyhood. It was a wooden pony galloping on ornate wooden rockers. I took this gaudy carousel escapee and painted an embellishment on it—a little hand-lettered, heart-shaped sign that read "Merritt's Pony." Schmaltzy? Never. It was just the kind of thing a one-time bohemian, lately family man would do in the joy of discovering he liked being a father. The horse still sits in our home. Merritt was the first of our children to ride it, but each of them in turn rode it as our family grew. Still, I suppose it will always remain Merritt's pony. It was a kind of symbol of family, the only icon of size that remains of Christmas 1988. In a way, Merritt was charging into the future on that little steed; indeed, she led all of us in a fast-lane gallop into a wonderful new home life.

Say no to the voice that tells you
you don't have time for the best things
in life...say yes to your simple visions.

Lemon Yellow Cake

Cake

Preheat oven to 375 degrees
Bake time 25 minutes

1 small package lemon Jell-O
2 1/4 cups cake flour
1 1/2 cups sugar
3/4 cup shortening
3/4 cup milk
2 1/2 teaspoons baking powder
1 teaspoon salt
1 teaspoon vanilla extract
1/2 teaspoon almond extract
3 large eggs

Topping

1 cup powdered sugar
1 cup brown sugar
1 lemon rind, grated
Juice of two lemons

Mix topping ingredients. While cake is still hot, puncture with fork and pour topping mixture over it

Grease and flour two 9-inch round cake pans. Into large bowl, measure all ingredients. With mixer at low speed, beat ingredients until well-mixed, scraping bowl with rubber spatula. Increase speed to high; beat 2 minutes, occasionally scraping bowl. Pour batter into pans. Bake 25 minutes or until toothpick comes out clean.

THOMAS KINKADE

That year I gave Nanette a miniature oil painting just as I had done the two previous years. But in 1988 I gave her a picture of a tree covered in heavy snow, and down in the valley far below were the twinkling lights of Placerville. No one can help but be impressed by the size of a Rembrandt canvas. But that little miniature was just the right gift for Nanette, for in its small frame it pictured all three miracles of Christmas 1988. Miracle number one was the town itself. The painting was of Placerville, where the unveiling had given me a certainty of God's direction and providence in my life. Miracle number two was the picture of that Christmas snow where the ski trip of a father and his young daughter had been a journey to the center of life. Miracle number three was the lights of Placerville, which told me of the direction that my life and art would forever take.

As she unwrapped the small four-by-six-inch painting, I said to her, "Honey, that tree is us—our family. We are growing strong. We will grow ever stronger with God's help, in spite of storms and troubles. Through the seasons of our lives, that tree is us."

We drank a pot of Christmas tea, while we played with Merritt and waited for her grandparents to arrive. But we knew somehow that—although the Kinkades had always loved God—our family had been born in a brand-new way that Christmas Day.

Christmas is finding a balance in the year

that we can look upon with fondness.